Simplicity
&
Silence

Look for these topics in the
Everyday Matters Bible Studies for Women

Acceptance	Mentoring
Bible Study & Meditation	Outreach
Celebration	Prayer
Community	Reconciliation
Confession	Sabbath & Rest
Contemplation	Service
Faith	Silence
Fasting	Simplicity
Forgiveness	Solitude
Gratitude	Stewardship
Hospitality	Submission
Justice	Worship

Simplicity & Silence

Spiritual Practices
FOR EVERYDAY LIFE

HENDRICKSON
PUBLISHERS

**Everyday Matters Bible Studies for Women—
Simplicity & Silence**

Printed in the United States of America

First Printing — November 2013

Contents

Silence

Holy Habits

Spiritual Practices for Everyday Life

Everyday life today is busier and more distracting than it has ever been before. While cell phones and texting make it easier to keep track of children and each other, they also make it harder to get away from the demands that overwhelm us. Time, it seems, is a shrinking commodity. But God, the Creator of time, has given us the keys to leading a life that may be challenging but not overwhelming. In fact, he offers us tools to do what seems impossible and come away refreshed and renewed. These tools are called spiritual practices, or spiritual disciplines.

Spiritual practices are holy habits. They are rooted in God's word, and they go back to creation itself. God has hardwired us to thrive when we obey him, even when it seems like his instructions defy our "common sense." When we engage in the holy habits that God has ordained, time takes on a new dimension. What seems impossible is actually easy; it's easy because we are tapping into God's resources.

The holy habits that we call spiritual practices are all geared to position us in a place where we can allow the Holy Spirit to work in us and through us, to grant us power and strength to do the things we can't do on our own. They take us to a place where we can become intimate with God.

While holy habits and everyday life may sound like opposites, they really aren't. As you learn to incorporate spiritual practices into your life, you'll find that everyday life is easier. At the same time, you will draw closer to God and come to a place where you can luxuriate in his rich blessings. Here is a simple example. Elizabeth Collings hated running household errands. Picking up dry cleaning, doing the grocery shopping, and chauffeuring her kids felt like a never-ending litany of menial chores. One day she had a simple realization that changed her life. That day she began to use her "chore time" as a time of prayer and fellowship with God.

Whenever Elizabeth walked the aisle of the supermarket, she prayed for each person who would eat the item of food she selected. On her way to pick up her children, she would lay their lives out before God, asking him to be there for them even when she couldn't. Each errand became an opportunity for fellowship with God. The chore that had been so tedious became a precious part of her routine that she cherished.

The purpose of these study guides is to help you use spiritual practices to make your own life richer, fuller, and deeper. The series includes twenty-four spiritual practices that are the building blocks of Christian spiritual formation. Each practice is a "holy habit" that has been modeled for us in the Bible. The practices are acceptance, Bible study and meditation, celebration, community, confession, contemplation, faith, fasting, forgiveness, gratitude, hospitality, justice, mentoring, outreach, prayer, reconciliation, Sabbath and rest, service, silence, simplicity, solitude, stewardship, submission, and worship.

As you move through the practices that you select, remember Christ's promise in Matthew 11:28–30:

Come to me, all of you who are weary and carry heavy burdens. Take my yoke upon you. Let me teach you, because I am humble and gentle at heart, and you will find rest for your souls. For my yoke is easy to bear, and the burden I give you is light.

Introduction

to the Practice of Simplicity & Silence

Simplicity. Silence. The very words themselves soothe, quiet, calm. They conjure visions of the beach at sunset, a mother caressing her sleeping child, a little boy sitting on a rock with his fishing rod waiting for a catch. Seems like another world, doesn't it?

Life has never been more stressful or fast-paced than it is today. With the great changes in technology that we've seen over the last two decades, life is utterly different today. The Internet has turned the world into a global village. Between Facebook, cell phones, texting and e-mail, you are always connected—perhaps more than you'd like.

As a society, America is on sensory overload. A simple evening dinner with the family is often something that has to be arranged in advance. For most people, a quiet walk includes using an iPod. And even a drive to the grocery store is no guarantee of a few minutes just to *be*. Cell phones and texting make it possible to be in conversation every minute of the day! It seems like simplicity and silence are quickly becoming as obsolete as phone booths and Walkmans.

So what does the Bible say about this phenomenon? Do we need simplicity? Is there any value in silence? In her powerful article "Two of Me" in the *Everyday Matters Bible for Women*, Mindy Caliguire says that the spiritual practice of simplicity is a way of life in which we truly assess what God's priorities are, not just our own. In Luke 6:29, Jesus says, "If someone demands your coat, offer your shirt also." He urges his followers not to store up treasures on earth where they can get used or lost or stolen, but to store our treasures in heaven. That's about things, but what about our time? Are we willing to give our time away? In many ways, that is more precious than our possessions. And if we give our time away to others, when will there be time to get everything done that needs to be accomplished? Simplicity isn't so simple after all, or so it seems.

The study on the practice of simplicity that follows focuses on our relationship to our priorities and our possessions. They point us in the direction of a simpler life that is not necessarily less busy or demanding. Sometimes simplicity is an attitude rather than a lifestyle.

Silence is the other spiritual practice that you will be studying in four sessions. In these chapters, you will experience what Jesus meant when he suggested that he and his disciples "go off by ourselves to find a quiet place." Sometimes the noise we experience doesn't come from the outside; it is the noise in our minds that has no volume control. This, too, is addressed in the Word, and as you explore the experience of Elijah, you will learn how God wants us to deal with distractions, inside and out.

" 'Tis the gift to be simple, 'tis the gift to be free; 'tis the gift to come down where we ought to be," says the old Shaker song. As you read, ponder, pray, and learn about simplicity and silence, may the Lord bring you closer to where you want to be and where he wants you to be.

Simplicity

CHAPTER 1

First Things First

Seek First the Kingdom of God

"And don't be concerned about what to eat and
what to drink. Don't worry about such things.
These things dominate the thoughts of unbelievers
all over the world, but your Father already knows
your needs. Seek the Kingdom of God above all
else, and he will give you everything you need."

LUKE 12:29-31

For this study, read Luke 12:22–34.

On the face of it, simplicity ought to be a simple concept
for Christians to understand and live out. After all, Jesus
plainly instructed us, "Don't be concerned about what you
eat or drink," and on more than one occasion he actually
demanded simplicity of us: "Unless you turn from your sins
and become like little children, you will never get into the
Kingdom of Heaven" (Matthew 18:3).

Living the life of simplicity, however, is anything but simple
for most Christians. Oftentimes, we don't even seem to
understand what it means. Life can so easily become, as a

contemporary songwriter put it, "complicated." It doesn't take much to complicate life. A delightful young child who turns into a stubborn, sullen, recalcitrant teen. A missed promotion. A spouse who becomes more and more distant. A bad diagnosis.

But sometimes we allow things to get in the way between us and God—and that's when life gets really complicated. Money, cares, ambitions, greed, desires, fears, and jealousy can all insert themselves where they do not belong. Underneath those complications our motives seep out, and if we are truthful, often they are not pretty.

At the core, a complex and complicated life often signals that we are trying to fill a void within—the God-shaped void—with something other than Christ. Instead of trusting God to provide, we take matters into our own hands.

- Instead of resting in God's care, we worry.

- Rather than living with enough, we seek more.

- Rather than keeping God the center of our lives, we substitute our possessions, or a job or prestige.

Simplicity, as Jesus tells us, is about removing those extraneous things that come between us and God. God did not intend that what we eat, drink, or wear should be primary matters of concern. He knows what we need. But first and foremost, our task as Christians is to seek the Kingdom of God and his righteousness. As Jesus points out, the things of God—his presence, his peace, his salvation—are more important than the things of this world.

Simplicity, then, is the antidote to our complicated lives, and it is a foundational principle of the Bible:

- God insists on being first, and honors those who keep him first.

- His law is based on keeping him first.

- Difficulties and punishment are the result of not keeping him first, of putting other people or things ahead of God.

As E. Stanley Jones, a missionary to India, said: "Evil is always complex, roundabout, tangled. Goodness is always a reduction of life to simplicity." And Dietrich Bonhoeffer wrote in *The Cost of Discipleship*, "The life of discipleship can only be maintained as long as nothing is allowed to come between Christ and ourselves—neither the law, nor personal piety, nor even the world." To be content with what we have is central to abiding in Christ and for living the life we were intended to have as Christians.

The extent to which you are content with life is directly related to whether you are in proper relationship with God. Reflect on the Scripture: "Give all your worries and cares to God, for he cares about you" (1 Peter 5:7).

As you study this chapter, think about situations where your life has become complicated. Reflect on what is really going on. Is it the situation that is complicating things—or is it you?

1. In Luke 22–34, Jesus says not to worry or be afraid; he also says to build up our treasures in heaven. How does that relate to simplicity in our lives? What are your fears? Where are you building up your treasures?

2. What does it mean to seek first the Kingdom of God and his righteousness?

3. In what ways have you allowed extraneous things to come between you and God? Do you know why? Examine your motives.

4. In Luke 12:32, Jesus says that it gives our Father great happiness to give us the Kingdom. Do you believe in your heart of hearts that God loves you that much? If not, why don't you?

5. Identify one thing you can do this week to simplify your life.

Points to Ponder

- David writes, "The LORD is my shepherd; I have all that I need" (Psalm 23:1). What does this mean to you? How is the Lord your shepherd? Do you feel you have all that you need (not necessarily what you want)?

- Jesus asked his disciples, "Can all your worries add a single moment to your life?" (Matthew 6:27). What are you worried about? How can you give these over to God?

"Seek the Kingdom of God above all else, and live righteously, and he will give you everything you need." (Matthew 6:33)

Prayer

Almighty God, our heavenly Father, who dost feed the birds and clothe the flowers, and who carest for us as a father for his children: We beseech thee of thy tender goodness to save us from distrust and vain self-concern; that with unwavering faith we may cast our every care on thee, and live in daily obedience to thy will; through thy beloved Son, Jesus Christ our Lord.
　　—Austrian Church Order, 1571

Add your prayer in your own words.

Amen.

Put It into Practice

Look back on your week and choose one area where life has grown complicated. Has anything come between you and God?

Take-away Treasure

God will provide for our needs. Remember that worry, fear, and "trying to make things happen" on our own are symptoms of a life that is out of God-control.

CHAPTER 2

Stuff and More Stuff

Craving Money, Wealth, and Possessions

Jesus looked around and said to his disciples,
"How hard it is for the rich to enter the Kingdom
of God!" This amazed them. But Jesus said
again, "Dear children, it is very hard to enter
the Kingdom of God. In fact, it is easier for a
camel to go through the eye of a needle than for
a rich person to enter the Kingdom of God!"

MARK 10:23-25

For this study, read Mark 10:17–25.

Among the most moving accounts of the early church are
those that describe the responsibility that Christians felt
toward one another. The book of Acts highlights how the
communities loved Christ and expressed that love, and
how it worked its way out in Christian character. In Acts
4:32, we are told: "All the believers were united in heart and
mind. And they felt that what they owned was not their
own, so they shared everything they had." The apostles had

testified so powerfully to the resurrection of the Lord Jesus that we are told in Acts 4:33 that "God's great blessing was upon them all."

As if to underscore the vibrancy of this community of believers, the writer of Acts reiterates the character of these new followers of Jesus. Christians sold their property and brought the proceeds to the apostles to be shared with those who had little or nothing: "There were no needy people among them, because those who owned land or houses would sell them and bring the money to the apostles to give to those in need" (Acts 4:34–35). For the early Christians, these actions were evidence of their utter abandonment to God and his Kingdom and to looking out for the needs of others.

But there were also pretenders—those who talked a fine game but kept a tight fist around their riches.

Meet Ananias and Sapphira. This couple was a part of the Christian community, people of means who were no doubt used to feeling competitive with other wealthy folks. They, too, sold land to give to give the money to the apostles, but unlike the others mentioned in Scripture, Ananias did something repugnant, as Acts 5:2 explains: "He brought part of the money to the apostles, claiming it was the full amount. With his wife's consent, he kept the rest."

The response to this is chilling: "Then Peter said, 'Ananias, why have you let Satan fill your heart? You lied to the Holy Spirit, and you kept some of the money for yourself. The property was yours to sell or not sell, as you wished. And after selling it, the money was also yours to give away.

How could you do a thing like this? You weren't lying to us but to God!'" As soon as he heard Peter's words, Ananias instantly fell dead.

Three hours later, when Sapphira arrived home and also lied to the church, she too fell dead instantly after Peter's rebuke: "How could the two of you of you even think of conspiring to test the Spirit of the Lord like this? The young men who buried your husband are just outside the door, and they will carry you out, too." We are told in verse 11 that "great fear gripped the entire church."

One of the seven deadly sins, greed almost always involves duplicity and deceit. It is often seductive and secretive. It can be open and corrosive and can lead to jealousy and envy. It is usually motivated by concern for what others think of us and our desire to be perceived in a particular way while holding on to what we have.

As a form of idolatry, greed is always deadly. In fact, God places greed on a par with sexual immorality and impurity. "So put to death the sinful, earthly things lurking within you. Have nothing to do with sexual immorality, impurity, lust, and evil desires," advises the apostle Paul in Colossians 3:5–6. "Don't be greedy, for a greedy person is an idolater, worshiping the things of this world. Because of these sins, the anger of God is coming." Remember Ananias and Sapphira.

> *As you think about this topic, be honest with yourself about those instances where your reliance on God may be lacking and where you may be more like the rich man that Jesus spoke of in the Gospels than you thought.*

Have you ever made a pledge to a building fund or contributed to a shower gift not because of God's prompting but because you felt you needed to keep up with others who were donating?

1. Do a study of the use of the word "greed" in the Bible (look in a concordance or search online). How does God view greed?

2. Consider the biblical admonitions about greed in Exodus 20:17 and James 4:1–11. What do these Scripture verses say to you?

3. Read the account of Gahazi, the servant of Elisha, in 2 Kings 5. Are there times when you have corrupted God's holy work with your own greed?

4. Does God hate rich people? How would you explain the words of Jesus in his response to the rich young ruler (Mark 10:17–21) and the parable of the rich man (Luke 12:13–21)? What is Jesus really saying?

5. Memorize (or re-memorize) Psalm 23 in the New Living Translation (or another modern translation that you prefer). Meditate on David's words about God's provision when we keep him at the center of our lives. Ask God to make you aware of greed in your life.

Enjoy what you have rather than desiring what you don't have. Just dreaming about nice things is meaningless—like chasing the wind. (Ecclesiastes 6:9)

Points to Ponder

The book of Proverbs offers frank assessments of the impact of greed on our lives. Read the following passages and consider the main warnings in these passages. How do they apply to your life?

- Proverbs 1:10–19

- Proverbs 15:27

- Proverbs 21:25–27

- Proverbs 28:20–22

- Proverbs 28:24–27

"Beware! Guard against every kind of greed. Life is not measured by how much you own." (Luke 12:15)

Prayer

God, of your goodness give me yourself for you are sufficient for me. I cannot properly ask anything less, to be worthy of you. If I were to ask less, I should always be in want. In you alone, do I have all. —Julian of Norwich

Lord, you have made me rich indeed, abounding in your grace, mercy, and salvation. Let me remember, with a thankful and reverent heart, all you have done.

Add your prayer in your own words.

Amen.

Put It into Practice

Ask God to take from you, in the words of Edmund Grindal, "the care of earthly vanities" and to make you "content with necessities and to keep your heart from delighting in honors, treasures and pleasures of this life."

Take-away Treasure

God will provide for our needs, so we need not strive or worry. We must seek more of him in order to receive more from him.

Idol Hearts

Solomon Foolishness

The Lord was very angry with Solomon, for his heart
had turned away from the Lord, the God of Israel.

1 KINGS 11:9

For this study, read 1 Kings 11:1–13.

God speaks to us. He commands us, he pleads with us, he
makes promises, he cajoles, he warns, he questions us. He
reveals himself in Scripture and tells us what is to happen
long before it ever comes to pass. Whatever else can be said
about him, he is not silent.

He appeared to Solomon in a dream at Gibeon. He asked
Solomon, son of the beloved King David, "What do you
want? Ask, and I will give it to you!" (1 Kings 3:5). This time
Solomon, who would build the temple of the Lord, seemed
to pass the test: he asked for wisdom to properly govern his
people.

But this same Solomon, who is widely regarded as the wis-
est and wealthiest person who has ever lived, turned away

from God in his old age and worshipped idols—false gods, objects of worship that were not the Lord of the universe, certainly not the God of the Bible. For this, Solomon would lose his kingdom. What was behind Solomon's sad downfall? He stopped listening to God and started listening to his foreign wives.

Among his seven hundred wives and three hundred concubines were many foreign women—women who did not worship the God of Israel, women Solomon was told in 1 Kings 11:2 not to marry, "because they will turn your hearts to their gods."

What God warned him about came to pass. First Kings 11:5 tells us that "in his old age" Solomon's heart became so corrupt that his wives "turned his heart to worship other gods instead of being completely faithful to the LORD His God as his father David." He "did what was evil in the LORD's sight."

What was so evil? Yes, Solomon worshipped God—but he also worshipped Ashtoreth, the fertility goddess of the Sidonians, and Molech, described as "the detestable god of the Ammonites," and Chemosh. Worship of Ashtoreth involved bizarre sexual practices and temple prostitution. Worship of Molech and Chemosh often involved parents sacrificing their infant children by placing them in flames to be burned to death to appease the so-called "god." The term "evil" doesn't begin to cover the depth of the depravity involved in such cultic worship.

Perhaps Solomon thought he was just being a good politician by indulging his foreign wives, some of whom came from rival nations or subjugated areas. If so, he was wrong.

The important thing to know about idols is that they are silent. Unlike the real God, they are just stone or wood or metal. Statues. Sculptures. They are created objects. No matter how hard you try to listen to them, they will not speak to you.

One thing, however, is certain: If you are listening to idols, it is a sure sign that you have stopped listening to God. This is the heart of idolatry. And this can mean disaster. Can you think of any "idols" in your life? What "voices" have you been listening to; what pastimes have you put in God's stead; what habits or practices or people or things have attained sacrosanct status in your life? Money? Youth? Sex? Fame? Hobbies? Work? TV? Food? Sports? Fashion? The list can be almost endless.

Idolatry is a form of greed: you are stealing the worship due the true God to give yourself to something else in order to gain something you think you want. That complicates life immeasurably—and it invites destruction.

The antidote to idolatry is to simplify life by removing the "idols" you may have become devoted to in place of God.

As you study this chapter, think about situations where your life has become complicated because of "idols" and how you might remove them.

1. What things have become idols in your life? Meditate on the warning of Paul to the Colossians (read Colossians 3:1–11).

2. The writer of Ecclesiastes cautions that those who love money will never have enough (5:10). Why is that the case?

3. How often do you "think about the things of heaven, not the things of earth" (Colossians 3:2)? What hinders your thinking more about the things of heaven?

4. What is one way you can work to remove that hindrance this week?

Points to Ponder

Read Ephesians 5:1–5.

- What does it mean to "live a life filled with love"?

- How do we follow "the example of Christ"?

Read Deuteronomy 6:5–10.

- Is it possible that is God "jealous" of anything in your life?

- Are both you and your loved ones following after him?

But let me say this, dear brothers and sisters: The time that remains is very short. So from now on, those with wives should not focus only on their marriage. Those who weep or who rejoice or who buy things should not be absorbed by their weeping or their joy or their possessions. Those who use the things of the world should not become attached to them. For this world as we know it will soon pass away. (1 Corinthians 7:29–31)

Prayer

Ask God to simplify your life and to take his rightful place in your heart. Ask him to purify your desires, alleviate your fears, loosen your hold on possessions, and remove the idols in your life.

> Almighty God, who knowest our necessities before we ask, and our ignorance in asking: Set free thy servants from all anxious thoughts for the morrow; give us contentment with thy good gifts; and confirm our faith that according as we seek thy kingdom, thou wilt not suffer us to lack any good thing; through Jesus Christ our Lord.
> —St. Augustine

Add your prayer in your own words.

Amen.

Put It into Practice

Ask God to reveal to you any forms of idolatry in your life and pray for him to remove them.

Take-away Treasure

By seeking God, by turning from self and the vain things of this world, it is possible to walk worthy of Christ.

CHAPTER 4

Toward a Life of Simplicity

Advice from Peter, James, and Paul

I have learned how to be content with whatever
I have. I know how to live on almost nothing
or with everything. I have learned the secret of
living in every situation, whether it is with a full
stomach or empty, with plenty or little. For I can do
everything through Christ, who gives me strength.

PHILIPPIANS 4:11–13

For this study, read Philippians 4:6–13.

"Yes, but . . ."

We have seen that simplicity is a key element of the Christian life—a necessary "discipline." But is it really possible to make simplicity a core discipline in our lives? Is it really possible to live a life of simplicity in this complex age?

Certainly we know it is possible to make a stab at reducing life to its simplest, curbing our dependence on material goods, getting rid of idols, invoking self-control, operating with restraint, giving more than we take, reducing our worrying, and cutting out pessimism. But is it really possible to live out that life of simplicity in Christ—and succeed over a lifetime? Won't the weeds of this life choke out the flowers of simplicity that bloom in our lives, until simplicity becomes just another good idea that starts out well but eventually winds up being shelved—like losing that extra twenty pounds on the exercise bike or reading fifteen chapters of the Bible every day?

Is it really possible? Yes.

Actually, it is not only possible; Peter tells us that it is impossible to truly live unless we live a simple godly life in Christ. Moreover, in 2 Peter 1:3, he tells us that "God has given us everything we need for living a godly life."

He does not, however, promise it will be easy. When we get rid of our idols, when we put away our greed, when we don't let worry and fear define us or paralyze us, when we put away the things of the flesh, we will likely experience some "pushback" from family or friends—and certainly from the Enemy. But it becomes possible to simplify life by doing everything through Christ, says Paul in Philippians, as he gives you the strength.

Think of the advantages we already have just because we are people of The Way! Peter tells us that the very fact that God has allowed us to know him, that he has drawn us to him, that we have received the gift of a Savior—and we don't have to work to try to save ourselves (as if we ever could!)— are incomparable gifts.

We also have every promise he has made to us—he will never leave us or forsake us; he has plans for us for our good and a hopeful future; he will provide, and many more— promises that Peter says allow us to actually share in God's divine nature and live above the level of corruption and mediocrity of this world (2 Peter 1:4). Do not underestimate what God has provided and is ready to give us.

As Jean-Pierre de Caussade, a French priest in the eighteenth century, tells us in *Self-Abandonment to Divine Providence*: "At every moment, God's Will produces what is needful for the task at hand, and the simple soul, instructed by faith, finds everything as it should be and wants neither more nor less than whatever it has."

Jesus sat down near the collection box in the Temple and watched as the crowds dropped in their money. Many rich people put in large amounts. Then a poor widow came and dropped in two small coins. Jesus called his disciples to him and said, "I tell you the truth, this poor widow has given more than all the others who are making contributions. For they gave a tiny part of their surplus, but she, poor as she is, has given everything she had to live on." (Mark 12:41–44)

> *As you study this chapter, remember what James tells us: "If you want to be a friend of the world, you make yourself an enemy of God" (James 4:4).*

1. Read the story of the widow's gift in Mark 12:41–44. Meditate on this simple story, considering what motivated the widow's actions. Could you do the same? How?

2. Consider Paul's admonitions to Timothy regarding money and contentment (read 1 Timothy 6:6–10). Are you content? Do you feel you have enough or do you lust for more, even when it's not needed?

3. Peter encourages us to realize that we have been given everything we need to live a godly life (read 2 Peter 1:3–7). What promises has God given us? Explore the practices that supplement our faith.

4. Do you agree with James (read 1:9) that believers who are poor have something to boast about because God has honored the poor?

5. Meditate on James 1:11. What does this mean to you?

6. Memorize Philippians 4:6–7 in the New Living Translation (or a translation you prefer). What are you worried about? What can you leave in God's hands?

Not that I was ever in need, for I have learned how to be content with whatever I have. (Philippians 4:11)

Points to Ponder

Paul's letter to the Philippians was written while Paul was imprisoned, late in his ministry. But despite his situation, he fills his letter with gratitude and joy for the love and support shown to him by the church in Philippi.

- How can he be so joyful when he's a prisoner and being persecuted? Read his words in Philippians 4:4–9.

- Can you apply his guidance to your life? Be specific.

- Read 1 Timothy 6:6–10 and meditate on Paul's hard words about money and wealth. Have you run after worldly gain? How do you view money? Can you be content with what you currently have?

By his divine power, God has given us everything we need for living a godly life. (2 Peter 1:3)

Prayer

Ask Jesus to strengthen you, to put away all anxiety and distress, to never be led astray by longings or useless preoccupations or by greed.

O God our God, grant us grace to desire you with our whole heart, so that desiring you we may seek and find you; and so finding you, may love you; and loving you, may hate those sins which separate us from you, for the sake of Jesus Christ our Lord. —St. Anselm

My God, here am I, my heart devoted to you. Fashion me according to your heart. —Brother Lawrence

Lord Jesu, I give Thee my body, my soul, my substance, my fame, my friends, my liberty, and my life; dispose of me, and of all that is mine, as it seemeth best to Thee, and to the glory of Thy blessed Name. Be Thou a light unto mine eyes, music to mine ears, sweetness to my taste, and a full contentment to my heart. Be Thou my sunshine in the day, my food at the table, my repose in the night, my clothing in nakedness, and my succour in all necessities. —Bishop Cosin

Add your prayer in your own words.

Amen.

Put It into Practice

The five keys to living a simple godly life are:

1. Take hold of God's promises in faith.

2. Don't worry about problems.

3. Tell God what you need and thank him for what he has done.

4. Fix your thoughts on what is true and honorable, right and pure, lovely and admirable (see Philippians 4:8).

5. Supplement your faith first with a generous dose of moral excellence, then add to it knowledge, then self-control, then patient endurance of hardship, then patient endurance of other people with godliness, then with brotherly affection, then with love for everyone.

Take-away Treasure

Grant me, O Lord, to know what I ought to know, to love what I ought to love, to praise what delights You the most, to value what is precious in Your sight, to hate what is offensive to you. Amen. —Thomas à Kempis

Notes / Prayer Requests

Notes / Prayer Requests

Silence

CHAPTER 1

A Time to Be Silent

Finding a Quiet Place

"Let's go off by ourselves to a quiet
place and rest awhile."

MARK 6:31

For this study, read Mark 6:31–32.

Silence is a spiritual discipline. Most disciplines seem
obvious—things like meditation, fasting, prayer, and confession. But silence? Silence seems like a negative, a void we
try to fill as soon as it presents itself. How can nothing be
something? How can silence be filled unless we fill it?

That's the irony of silence. It is not something we are to fill.
Rather, silence is to be filled by God. Adele Calhoun, in the
Spiritual Disciplines Handbook, defines the discipline of
silence as "the regenerative practice of attending and listening to God in quiet, without interruption or noise. (Reading
is also listening to words.)"

It turns out that we are addicted to noise, to words, to distractions of all sorts. We fill our lives with television, radio,

computers, phones, music, even reading. It is as if we cannot tolerate life without distractions. How many of us eat in front of the television, or set the sleep function on our set to help us fall asleep to late night shows?

Most of us are plugged into at least one personal electronic device, be it a phone, a computer, a tablet, an MP3 player, or any of the myriad of new gadgets available today. The irony is that while these devices can enhance our daily lives, they also allow us to feel we are being silent—all the while stuffing ourselves with texting, e-mails, games, news, magazines, books, movies, and music. Never underestimate the impact of these "conveniences" on our lives, including our spiritual health. We carry in these small devices entire worlds of noise and distraction.

Silence is foundational to all the other spiritual disciplines. It is often practiced with the discipline of solitude, since most people find solitude necessary to successfully enter into silence. Consider the example of Jesus, who regularly withdrew from the crowds and retired to a private place where he could find silence, so he could pray, rest, and be refreshed. These were often occasions of intense spiritual battles as well, such as his temptation in the wilderness or his prayers in Gethsemane. Though he felt the pressure to serve the people who came to him for healing and for ministry, he recognized his need for solitude and silence in order to interact with his Father in the most intense and intimate ways.

But Jesus often withdrew to the
wilderness for prayer. (Luke 5:16)

As you study the discipline of silence, pray for God to point out the noise and distractions you invite into your life. Pray that he will show you the distractions that family, work, and church impose on your life. Pray that you surrender the distractions and welcome the times of silence—times when you rest in his love, when he nurtures you and enjoys your attention.

1. Study the example of Jesus as he withdrew from the crowds. Read the following verses in the context of the bigger story and note the role that silence—coming apart from noise and distraction—plays in these situations.

- The Temptation in Matthew 4:1–8 and Luke 4:1–8:

- The Garden of Gethsemane in Matthew 26:36–44 and Mark 14:32–44:

- Other occasions in Matthew 14:23; Mark 1:35; 6:46; Luke 4:42; 6:12; and John 11:54:

2. When you get into your car to drive, turn off the radio and music devices. Keep them off while you drive. Invite God into the quiet. What did you experience?

3. List the specific distractions in your life, whatever prohibits you from experiencing silence (children, family, entertainments, or work):

4. Are you encouraging others, such as your children, to use noise as a distraction? Are their lives filled with things like talking, music, games, movies, and television? Can you set an example for others of finding silence? Do you encourage others to be comfortable with the quiet? Can you sit with someone else in silence?

5. Develop a plan for being silent. Be practical and realistic. How can you do this?

6. What would happen if you turned off the television set?

Thou hast made us for thyself and restless is our heart until it comes to rest in Thee.
—*St. Augustine,* Confessions

Points to Ponder

- Memorize Isaiah 30:15 in the New Living Translation (or in your favorite translation). How does God's admonition relate to your own life?

- Meditate on these words from a beloved hymn by John Greenleaf Whittier. What does this say to you?

  With that deep hush subduing all
  Our words and works that drown
  The tender whisper of Thy call,
  As noiseless let Thy blessing fall
  As fell Thy manna down.
  Drop Thy still dews of quietness,
  Till all our strivings cease;
  Take from our souls the strain and stress,
  And let our ordered lives confess
  The beauty of Thy peace.

Only to sit and think of God,
Oh what a joy it is!
To think the thought, to breathe the Name,
Earth has no higher bliss!
—*Frederick William Faber, "My Father"*

Prayer

O Lord, the Scripture says, "There is a time for silence and a time for speech." Savior, teach me the silence of humility, the silence of wisdom, the silence of love, the silence that speaks without words, the silence of faith. Lord, lead me to silence my own heart that I may listen to the gentle movement of the Holy Spirit within me and sense the depths which are God.

—Source unknown, 16th century

O Lord Jesus Christ, who didst say to thine Apostles, "Come ye apart into a desert place and rest awhile," for there were many coming and going; grant, we beseech thee, to thy servants here gathered together, that they may rest awhile at this present time with thee. May they so seek thee, whom their souls desire to love, that they may both find thee and be found of thee.

—Richard Meux Benson

Add your prayer in your own words.

Amen.

Put It into Practice

Begin to practice the discipline of silence. In the first week, be silent five to ten minutes several times a day. Seek out a place of quiet; turn off all noise and distraction. Sometimes setting a timer can help you resist watching the clock. And you may need to practice recognizing the noise and distractions that can muddle your mind. Then welcome God's presence into the silence.

Take-away Treasure

Though noise has become our usual milieu and distraction is a common companion, God encourages us to accept his invitation to meet him in a place of silence.

CHAPTER 2

Silencing the Noise

Hold the Drama, Mama

> And after the earthquake there was a fire, but the
> LORD was not in the fire. And after the fire there
> was the sound of a gentle whisper. When Elijah
> heard it, he wrapped his face in his cloak and went
> out and stood at the entrance of the cave. And a
> voice said, "What are you doing here, Elijah?"
>
> 1 KINGS 19:12-13

For this study, read 1 Kings 18:1–19:13.

Noise is so pervasive in our lives that we aren't even aware of the clamor. We don't realize that we can't hear God. How is that?

The accounts of the prophet Elijah offer us some insight into how the Lord gets our attention. Elijah was the most theatrical of prophets. At God's direction, he repeatedly challenged the most wicked royal team in Israel's history, King Ahab and his notorious queen Jezebel. Elijah was a man of power at the complete bidding of God. And then, still under God's direction, Elijah would retreat—okay, he would run and hide from his enemies. His emotions would vacillate from the elation of a dramatic spiritual victory in God's name to periods of fear, defeat, and despair.

It was the goal of King Ahab and Queen Jezebel to turn Israel away from the worship of God to the worship of pagan god Baal. So Elijah challenged Ahab and the entire nation: You have to pick. If the Lord is God, follow him. If Baal is God, then follow him.

Elijah challenged the prophets of Baal to a battle of the sacrifices and the contest was spectacular—fire from heaven spectacular! Where the prophets of Baal failed, Elijah, as agent of the Lord God, was victorious. Naturally, Ahab and Jezebel were furious, vowing to kill Elijah. And despite the great display of God's power, Elijah became afraid and ran for his life, ultimately ending up hiding in a mountainous cave. Though God sent an angel to care for him, Elijah was depressed and filled with self-pity, complaining that he was the only remaining faithful person left in Israel.

In response, the Lord instructed Elijah to leave the cave and stand on the mountain. The Lord was going to pass by. First came a powerful wind that tore the mountain apart, but the Lord was not in the wind. Then came an earthquake, but the Lord was not in the earthquake. And then came a fire, but the Lord was not in the fire. And finally, when the wind, the earthquake, and the fire had passed, when the din had quieted, Elijah heard the sound of a gentle whisper. The Lord was in that whisper.

It was in the silence that Elijah could hear God. So it is with us. We are lured by drama and excitement when what is required is quiet, silence. Silence is critical to hearing. And

God wants us to listen. Only in listening can we recognize and receive God's comfort or determine God's direction and his intentions. So what prevents us from hearing?

Sometimes it's the distraction of our toys and devices that fill the air with noisy entertainments. And sometimes it's our work and all the pressures that tug at us, demanding attention. Maybe it's the pressing needs of our family—overscheduled afterschool activities, feeding, cleaning, shopping. Or worry: financial difficulties, health issues, loneliness, grief, troublesome relationships, or even natural disasters. Or perhaps the clamor comes from our own mouths: complaints, idle talk, arguing, bullying, or simple chatter just to keep the quiet at bay.

Nineteenth-century cleric and hymn writer Frederick W. Faber observed, "There is hardly ever a complete silence in our soul. God is whispering to us well-nigh incessantly. Whenever the sounds of the world die out in the soul, or sink low, then we hear these whisperings of God. He is always whispering to us, only we do not always hear, because of the noise, hurry, and distraction which life causes as it rushes on."

We must wait for God, long, meekly, in the
wind and wet, in the thunder and lightning, in
the cold and the dark. Wait, and he will come.
He never comes to those who do not wait.
—Frederick William Faber

> *As you study the discipline of silence,*
> *learn to listen for the whisper.*

1. In the midst of all the noise surrounding you, in what ways can you carve out space and time for silence in your life?

2. Ask God to make you aware of the occasions and reasons that you invite noise into your life. Keep a record of what God reveals to you: what you learn about yourself and any successes you have in pushing back the distractions and embracing God's presence.

3. What do you consider the most distracting parts of your life? Your family: spouse, children, in-laws? Your work? Your chores? Your studies? Write a paragraph describing the most intrusive distractions and frustrations.

4. Read the complete account of Elijah's life (1 Kings 16:29–34; 17:1–24; 18:1–45; 19:1–21; 21:1–29; 2 Kings 1:1–18; 2:1–12). Note especially his courageous faithfulness to God in his opposition to Ahab and Jezebel's wickedness—and his despondent periods as well. What stands out to you in these passages?

5. What happens when you turn off the television? Can you sense God's presence or hear his voice in the quiet?

Teach me, and I will keep quiet.
Show me what I have done wrong. (Job 6:24)

Points to Ponder

I waited patiently for the LORD to help me,
  and he turned to me and heard my cry. (Psalm 40:1)

• Memorize Psalm 27:7–8 in the New Living Translation (or your favorite translation).

• Does your heart respond like David's did?

Nothing in all creation is so like God as is stillness.
—Meister Eckhart

Prayer

Dearest Father God, thank you for being present. Thank you for your generous invitation to come apart from the noise to join you. Thank you for your patient waiting when I resist or when I can't hear your voice for the wind, the earthquake, or the fire. And thank you for your generous welcome into the place where sounds are silent but still filled with your praise. In your Son's holy name.

Add your prayer in your own words.

Amen.

Put It into Practice

Continue to practice the discipline of silence. In this second week, try to increase your times of silence to ten minutes a day, longer and more often if you're comfortable with it. The goal is to develop a habit that takes practice, practice, practice. Remember to turn off all the noise and put aside any distraction. Seek out a place of where you can be quiet and enter into God's presence. Be patient with yourself—it may take a bit of time to settle down. Attend to God and what he wants to give to you.

Silences are the only scrap of Christianity we have left.
—Søren Kierkegaard

Take-away Treasure

Cultivate the habit of noise awareness: learn to recognize the clamor and racket that you permit, indeed invite, into your life that muffles the voice of God.

Managing Your Tongue

Yak, Yak, Yak

If you claim to be religious but don't control
your tongue, you are fooling yourself,
and your religion is worthless.

JAMES 1:26

For this study, read James 3:2–12.

Today, a popular rebuke to those who use crude or profane language is, "Do you kiss your mother with that mouth?" The idea is that words can contaminate. Those of us who pursue a relationship with a holy God know this better than most people. Our speech might be considered a gateway sin: seemingly unimportant and harmless. But the Bible says otherwise. In fact our speech—the tongue—gets a lot of attention in the Bible.

Consider the sins of the tongue. Begin with the words that we use to serve ourselves. These include things like gossiping, tattling, lying, boasting, and arguing. How about indulging in innuendo or idle chatter? Or being a busybody, butting into other people's business? Or maybe upstaging others by stealing their thunder: have we ever ruined the end of someone else's story or spoiled the punch line of a joke?

Do we use words to make ourselves look clever or funny? A recent survey found that over a third of us admit that we've pretended to know about a news story in order to impress someone else. Expand on this: Do we ever pretend that we've read a particular book or listened to a particular speaker or watch a particular television show? And don't discount the temptation to be a consumer of gossip as delivered by entertainment shows, tabloid stories, and celebrity dish.

Then there are the words meant to hurt and demean others—sarcasm, flippancy, derision, scorn, ridicule, and disrespect. We use words to bully others, perhaps not intentionally, yet that is the result. And we tell crude jokes, in order to make ourselves seem witty and "with it."

Finally there are the words that disrespect and dishonor God. Call it cursing or blasphemy, it means using profanity and expletives to punctuate our speech. God specifically forbids this in his commandments. The King James Version cautions us not to "take the name of the LORD thy God in vain" (Exodus 20:7). *The Message* translates the verse: "No using the name of God, your God, in curses or silly banter; God won't put up with the irreverent use of his name." This begs the question: Does cursing include using the acronym "OMG"?

The discipline of silence is about managing our words, which includes shutting up as well as speaking up. The goal is a controlled tongue—that is, words well spoken: restrained, controlled, timely, and appropriate. Using words that are kind and positive and truthful.

In Matthew 12:33–37, Jesus is very clear about the words we use:

"A tree is identified by its fruit. If a tree is good, its fruit will be good. If a tree is bad, its fruit will be bad. You brood of snakes! How could evil men like you speak what is good and right? For whatever is in your heart determines what you say. A good person produces good things from the treasury of a good heart, and an evil person produces evil things from the treasury of an evil heart. And I tell you this, you must give an account on judgment day for every idle word you speak. The words you say will either acquit you or condemn you."

In his letter to the Philippians, Paul encouraged us to "fix your thoughts on what is true, and honorable, and right, and pure, and lovely, and admirable. Think about things that are excellent and worthy of praise" (4:8). If our thoughts are good, our speech will be good. And those good thoughts are nurtured in silence.

Silence promotes the Presence of God, avoids many harsh or proud words, and suppresses many dangers in the way of ridiculing or rashly judging our neighbors. Silence humbles the mind, and detaches it from the world. . . . If you are steadfast in keeping silence when it is not necessary to speak, God will preserve you from evil when it is right for you to talk. —François Fénelon

> *As you continue in your study on silence, think about how you can cultivate a good heart that produces good words.*

1. Read through the short book of James. What does James have to say about managing our speech, especially as it relates to living a godly life?

2. Practice holding your tongue. Monitor your conversations so that you become aware of your communications, by mouth or electronic means. What is one thing you can do this week to manage your own tongue?

3. Meditate on Exodus 20:1–17. Focus especially on the third commandment, verse 7, and reflect on your own speech. Does your speech honor God or disrespect him? Do you misuse his name?

4. When was the last time you sinned with your speech? Have you gossiped or used words to hurt someone else or misrepresent yourself? Did you speak out of turn or profane God's name, whether intentionally or not? Ask God to make you aware of these occasions and to teach you to tame your tongue.

5. What can be learned about managing our speech from Paul's admonitions in Ephesians 4:21–32?

6. Spend more time without the television on. Do you notice any difference in your life?

──────────── ❧ ────────────

If you are to be self-controlled in your speech, you must be self-controlled in your thinking. —François Fénelon

Points to Ponder

• Memorize Psalm 19:14 in the New Living Translation (or in your favorite translation). Hold these words close as you learn to tame your tongue.

> *May the words of my mouth*
> *and the meditation of my heart*
> *be pleasing to you,*
> *O Lord, my rock and my redeemer.*

- Using an online Bible or a concordance, research key words such as tongue, mouth, lips, speech, words, gossip, or whisperer, in several Bible translations if you can. Select passages that speak to your own life and compare the verse in various translations. Meditate on what can be learned about the godly life from various translations. For example, compare these five translations of Psalm 21:23:

If you keep your mouth shut, you will stay out of trouble. (NLT)

He who guards his mouth and his tongue keeps himself from calamity. (NIV)

Whoso keepeth his mouth and his tongue keepeth his soul from troubles. (KJV)

Whoever keeps his mouth and his tongue keeps himself out of trouble. (ESV)

Watch your words and hold your tongue; you'll save yourself a lot of grief. (MSG)

*Take control of what I say, O Lord,
and guard my lips! (Psalm 141:3)*

Prayer

Father, as we bless your name, we ask your help as we learn to discipline our speech. The apostle James has taught us to tame our tongues, so that the air is not filled with foolish chatter and our lives are not filled with chaos and unhappiness. Please teach us to embrace silence and by doing so, welcome your presence. In your holy name.

Add your prayer in your own words.

Amen.

Put It into Practice

Every day, continue your practice of the discipline of silence. Expand your commitment: consider setting aside one day where the goal is to be silent fifteen to thirty minutes. This week, focus on your words—spoken, written, and thought. Ask God to make you aware of any of your words that are not "true, and honorable, and right, and pure, and lovely, and admirable."

Take-away Treasure

Our personal speech is the most significant obstacle to enjoying the silence necessary for enjoying God's presence in our lives. By learning to curb our speech—to control our tongues—we make space for the silence.

CHAPTER 4

Embracing Silence

To Wait Patiently for the Lord

The Lord is good to those who depend on him,
to those who search for him.
So it is good to wait quietly
for salvation from the Lord.

LAMENTATIONS 3:25-26

For this study, read Lamentations 3:22–28.

For us today, silence is deafening. There is virtually no place we can go where we don't hear the sounds of civilization, be it the background hum of an air conditioner, the distant wail of a car alarm, the drone of the computer, or the sounds of neighbors simply living their lives—talking, mowing the lawn, playing music, listening to the ball game on the radio. Noise is so ever present in our lives that we are forced to be intentional about being silent.

The discipline of silence is not meant to be a chore or a punishment. It's meant to be an occasion of love, an act of worship, a time to wait and listen. It's an opportunity to restore our spiritual perspective and to pursue the will of

God. Most of all, silence gives us a chance to be with God, to hear him, to listen, and to respond.

In Lamentations, Jeremiah encourages us to wait quietly for the Lord, reminding us that "it is good for people to submit at an early age to the yoke of his discipline." Yes, spiritual disciplines are good things. Yet most of us don't voluntarily practice the discipline of silence. God extends an open invitation to us to unplug from our lives of noise and distraction, yet most of us don't accept his offer until we are backed into a corner. It is usually when we face a crisis—sickness, spiritual dryness, family problems, work issues, financial emergencies—that we find ourselves driven into silence and solitude to find the answers and solace we seek.

Are there benefits to practicing the discipline of silence? Absolutely!

- *Spiritual*—When we practice the disciple of silence, we become aware of and responsive to the Lord. God uses silence to make us aware of the corrosion and cracks that eat away at us, and he uses silence to provide healing and wholeness.

- *Physical*—In silence, our bodies are able to slow down. As we begin to relax, the heartbeat slows, the breathing slows. Without noise, without distractions, we become more mindful of our physical needs, capabilities, and even our limitations. Perhaps we shouldn't be surprised if at first the body's response to silence is to nap. It may be that sleep is one of our most pressing needs. So we can take a short nap, but after we awaken, we remain in the silence to meet God.

- *Mental*—Silence allows our minds to recalibrate. We get off the hamster wheel of worry, doubt, and frustration. It sets the stage so that when we leave the silence, we bring fresh clarity, wisdom, and creativity to our work and relationships.

- *Emotional*—In silence, our emotions are quieted and clarified, allowing us to see the truth about ourselves and our relationships. Is pride standing in the way of forgiveness? Is fear interfering with love? Is worry crippling creativity? Are relationships at risk because we are impaired spiritually? In silence comes peace, a peace that passes understanding.

So how do we make silence a regular part of our lives? We start by making an appointment. We make a commitment, set a time and a place, and then show up! We keep that appointment. It usually means starting small, with short periods of time—five minutes, perhaps once a day. Then as time goes by, we increase the length of time and the frequency. We unplug from everything—no electronics, no reading, just stillness. And we couple the discipline of silence with the discipline of solitude, to find that place where we can be alone and undisturbed. It can even be something as simple as Susannah Wesley's practice of pulling her apron up over her head to signal to her children that she was not to be disturbed as she prayed and read the Bible.

*God is our true Friend, who always gives us the
counsel and comfort we need. Our danger lies in
resisting Him; so it is essential that we acquire the
habit of hearkening to His voice, or keeping silence
within, and listening so as to lose nothing of what
He says to us. We know well enough how to keep
outward silence, and to hush our spoken words, but
we know little of interior silence.* —*François Fénelon*

**As you study this chapter, think about how you
can make silence a regular part of your life.
What is the noise you can do without?**

1. How can you make a specific plan for incorporating the
discipline of silence into a regular part of your life?

2. Turn off the television, the radio, and the music in your
home and simply listen. What do you hear after these intrusive noises have been silenced?

3. Find your own personal quiet place—perhaps where the only sounds are sounds of nature, or at least a place that offers solitude and privacy. Is there somewhere you can go on a regular basis to be silent?

4. List some Bible characters who withdrew from the noise and distraction and had a powerful encounter with God. Note the occasion or motivation for their actions and the results of the encounter. Some examples are Moses (Exodus 2:11–25; 3:1–10), David (1 Samuel 16:1–13), Elijah (1 Kings 17:1–7), and Paul (Acts 9:1–31).

5. Add a classic Christian journal or biography to your reading program to discover how God has worked in the lives of others who have mindfully made space for him. Have you read a journal or biography that really resonated with you? If so, what did you learn?

6. Now that you've been in the habit of turning off your television for a period of time, what have you discovered? If you started off in small time increments, have you increased the amount of no-TV time? If so, have you noticed a difference in your spiritual life?

Outward silence is indispensable for the cultivation and improvement of inner silence. —Madame Jeanne Guyon

---

Points to Ponder

- Memorize Psalm 62:5–8 in the New Living Translation (or your favorite translation).

- It is in the quiet that we discover the strength that God has provided for us. What are some specific ways you sense God's strength in your life?

Wait patiently for the LORD.
Be brave and courageous.
Yes, wait patiently for the LORD. (Psalm 27:14)

Prayer

O my Divine Master, teach me to hold myself in silence before you; to adore you in the depth of my being; to wait upon you always and never to ask anything of you but the fulfillment of your will. Teach me to let you act in me and form in me the simple prayer that says little but includes everything. Grant me this favor for the glory of your name. Amen. —Père Nicolas Grou

Add your prayer in your own words.

Amen.

Rest in the Lord; wait patiently for Him. In Hebrew, "Be silent in God, and let Him mold thee." Keep still, and He will mold thee to the right shape. —Martin Luther

Put It into Practice

In the fourth week, continue to practice the discipline of silence, using the time and frequency that works for you. The goal is not necessarily measurement. It is about the discipline of turning off the noise and blocking the distractions so that we are totally available to God. Consider expanding this time of silence to perhaps an hour or more at least one day of the week. And take advantage of a retreat center, a place apart where silence is expected and often required of retreatants.

Take-away Treasure

Seek the quiet; recognize and reject the noise and distractions of your life; learn to control your speech. Practicing the discipline of silence will not only bring you into God's presence and into his peace; it will also form the foundation for practicing many other spiritual disciplines, such as prayer, worship, forgiveness, simplicity, and solitude.

Notes / Prayer Requests

Notes / Prayer Requests

Leader's Guide

to Simplicity & Silence

Thoughts on Where to Meet

- If you have the chance, encourage each group member to host a gathering. But make sure your host knows that you don't expect fresh baked scones from scratch or white-glove-test-worthy surroundings. Set the tone for a relaxed and open atmosphere with a warm welcome wherever you can meet. The host can provide the space and the guests can provide the goodies.

- If you can't meet in homes, consider taking at least one of your meetings on the road. Can you meet at a local place where people from your community gather? A park or a coffee shop or other public space perhaps.

- If you meet in a church space, consider partnering with another local church group and take turns hosting. How can you extend your welcome outside your group?

Thoughts on Ways to Foster Welcome

- If many of your members have a hard time meeting due to circumstances, look for ways to work around it. Consider providing childcare if there are moms who have difficulty attending, or meet in an accessible space if someone who might want to join has a disability. Does a morning time work better? Could you meet as smaller groups and then get together as a larger group for an event? Be flexible and see how you can accommodate the needs of the group.

- Incorporate "get to know you" activities to promote sharing. Don't take yourselves too seriously and let your humor shine through.

Simplicity

Chapter 1: Luke 12:29 tells us not to worry about earthly things. Ask each member of your group to choose one worry that is on her mind and take a "worry vacation" from it for the next week. Each time she starts to worry about that issue, she should spend that time in prayer about it. At the start of your next session, ask each member to share that experience with the group. Any unexpected results?

Chapter 2: At the start of this session, ask each participant (including yourself) to remove one piece of jewelry or accessory she's wearing and to put it in her purse. Proceed with the session. At the end of the meeting, ask if the members missed wearing the item they had removed. Chances are, most of them won't even remember that they'd taken it off. This is a good picture of what it feels like to simplify our lives. Often, we don't miss things we thought we needed. Ask each member to take a life inventory of time and stuff to see if anything is getting in the way of a truly full life. How can they find ways to repurpose an abundance of stuff?

Chapter 3: We don't think much about idols today, but most of us do have them. Ask each member of the group if she recognized an idol in her life as she studied this lesson. What items were mentioned? Ask the group to be mindful in the coming week of their "idols" and to think about ways to remove them from their "thrones."

Chapter 4: Ask each member to name the area of her life that she most needs to simplify, and then ask the group to suggest ways that she can begin to streamline.

Silence

Chapter 1: Open this session with a prayer. After the prayer is over, remain silent for one minute. The group will probably look to you to begin discussion, but just smile. At the end of 60 seconds, ask the group how it felt to be silent for one minute. Was it uncomfortable? Did it seem like more than just a minute? Consider practicing a minute of silence after the opening prayer at each of the four sessions. Does that minute of silence shift from a time of discomfort to a welcome moment of quiet meditation? Ask the members if their response to that minute has changed over time.

Chapter 2: Sometimes the noise in our heads is louder than the noise we hear. Often we get so used to that interior noise that we forget we're being assaulted by it. Ask the members what noises go through their heads that are difficult to "turn off." Discuss ways to be mindful of that "noise in our heads" and how to turn down the volume. Suggest that members kneel to pray once a day and at your next meeting, ask if kneeling helped to silence the distracting interior noise during prayer.

Chapter 3: Did you know that the average adult woman speaks an average of 20,000 words every day? (The average adult male speaks about 7,000 words every day.) Controlling our speech may well be the most difficult challenge in the study of silence. During this session, ask each member to identify an area of her life or a relationship with a specific person that would be enhanced if she was more mindful of her speech with that person. Ask what she can do to measure her words before she engages in talk that could be damaging. Follow up next week to learn each member's experience with this exercise.

Chapter 4: Discuss with the group various ways to incorporate silence into your lives in unusual ways. Some may choose to refrain from using their cell phones or iPods when they're out. Or when driving, turn off the radio and any communication devices. Next week, follow up to see if some unexpected results emerged.

Incorporating Other Practices

- *Lift your voices.* Integrate worship throughout the study. Find songs that speak about simplicity and silence.

- *Commit to lift each other up in prayer.* You may want to have a prayer walk as part of seeing opportunities to serve in your community, or prayer partners who might be able to meet at other times.

- *Dig deep into the word.* Take the study at your own pace, but consider including passages for participants to read in between meetings. The *Everyday Matters Bible for Women* has a wealth of additional resources.

- *Give thanks.* Gratitude reenergizes us for humble service. Assemble a group list of one hundred reasons to give thanks.

EVERYDAY MATTERS BIBLE STUDIES
for women

Spiritual practices for everyday life

Acceptance	Mentoring
Bible Study & Meditation	Outreach
Celebration	Prayer
Community	Reconciliation
Confession	Sabbath & Rest
Contemplation	Service
Faith	Silence
Fasting	Simplicity
Forgiveness	Solitude
Gratitude	Stewardship
Hospitality	Submission
Justice	Worship

HENDRICKSON PUBLISHERS

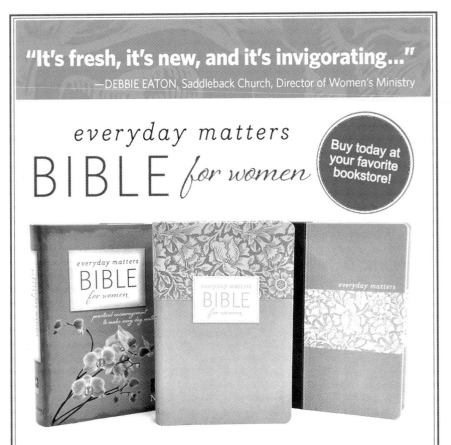